"The Power of Social Media Marketing for Small Business Growth"

((Georgia Ramos))

Text Copyright© 2023 By ((Georgia Ramos))

Table of Contents

Introduction

Welcome to a journey that promises to transform your small business into a thriving success story! In a world where social media has become the beating heart of connectivity, "The Power of Social Media Marketing for Small Business Growth" is your ultimate guide to harnessing the boundless potential of digital platforms to propel your enterprise to new heights.

Have you ever wondered how some small businesses seem to effortlessly captivate their audience, boost their brand, and skyrocket their sales through the magic of social media? Well, wonder no more! This book is your ticket to unveiling the secrets behind their extraordinary success.

In these pages, we will unlock the treasure chest of strategies, tips, and techniques that will not only demystify the world of social media but also empower you to navigate it confidently. Whether you're a seasoned entrepreneur looking to refresh your marketing game or a fresh-faced startup eager to make your mark, this book is tailor-made.

But here's the secret sauce – we won't drown you in jargon or bore you with technical jibber-jabber. Instead, we'll take you on a journey filled with real-world examples, relatable anecdotes, and practical advice you can immediately implement. It's like having a trusted friend guide you through the maze of hash tags, algorithms, and viral content, ensuring your small business shines brightly in the digital galaxy.

if you're ready to step into the exciting realm of social media marketing, where innovation meets strategy and creativity sparks growth, then grab a comfy chair, your favorites beverage, and dive into the adventure that is "The Power of Social Media Marketing for Small Business Growth." The opportunity to craft your success story begins right here, and we can make it a reality together—so don't merely dream; let's accomplish it together!

Chapter 1
The Digital Landscape Unveiled

In the vast expanse of the internet, a digital ecosystem has revolutionized how we communicate, interact, and conduct business. It's a landscape characterized by constant change, where trends rise and fall at the speed of a click, and small businesses are presented with unprecedented opportunities for growth and success. Welcome to the digital landscape, a place where the power of social media marketing for small business growth truly comes to life.

Understanding the Digital Landscape

To embark on a journey of harnessing the power of social media for your small business, it's crucial first to understand the lay of the land. The digital landscape is a dynamic, interconnected space encompassing various platforms, channels, and technologies. At its core are social media platforms—virtual communities where people share, interact, and engage with content.

The rise of social media has brought about a profound shift in how people communicate. It has democratized information, allowing anyone with an internet connection to become a publisher, influencer, or brand ambassador. Small businesses, in particular, have gained unprecedented access to their target audience. Even the smallest enterprises can compete globally with a well-crafted social media strategy.

The Impact on Modern Business

The impact of the digital landscape on modern business cannot be overstated. It has disrupted traditional marketing channels, challenged established business models, and rewritten the rules of customer engagement. In this age of information overload, consumers have become more discerning, demanding authenticity, relevance, and attention from the brands they choose to support.

Social media is not just a tool for marketing; it's a gateway to building meaningful relationships with your audience. It's where conversations happen, opinions are formed, and decisions are made. This offers an exclusive chance for small businesses to establish personal connections with potential customers, narrate their brand's story, and distinguish themselves in a competitive marketplace.

Why Small Businesses Need to Embrace Social Media

Why is it essential for small businesses to embrace social media marketing? The solution can be found in social media's growth, visibility, and impact.

Cost-Effective Marketing: Traditional advertising can be expensive and may yield different results than a well-executed social media campaign. Social media enables you to access a broad audience without incurring significant costs.

Targeted Marketing: Social media platforms offer advanced targeting capabilities, enabling you to connect with the appropriate audience using precisely tailored messages. This precision can significantly improve your conversion rates.

Brand Building:
Constructing a brand goes beyond merely having a logo and a captivating slogan; it involves establishing a uniform and unforgettable customer experience. Social media is a potent instrument in brand establishment, aiding in forming your brand's identity and storyline.

Customer Engagement: Customers expect to engage with brands on social media. They want to ask questions, provide feedback, and feel heard. Social media offers a space for immediate engagement, cultivating and strengthening customer loyalty.

Competitive Advantage: Many of your competitors are already on social media. To remain competitive, you need to be there too. Not only that, but you also need to stand out and offer something unique.

Measurable Results: Social media marketing offers extensive data and analytics, unlike traditional marketing methods.

You can monitor your campaign's effectiveness, assess return on investment, and base your decisions on data, enabling you to enhance your strategy.

The Ever-Evolving Landscape

One thing to remember is that the digital landscape is constantly in flux. What works today might not work tomorrow. New platforms emerge, algorithms change, and consumer behaviors evolve. Small businesses must be adaptable and open to continuous learning to succeed in this dynamic environment.

This book is your roadmap to navigating the ever-evolving digital landscape. We'll guide you through the intricacies of social media marketing, from defining your strategy to crafting compelling content, from understanding algorithms to measuring success. Whether you're a seasoned entrepreneur looking to refresh your marketing game or a fresh-faced startup eager to make your mark, this book is tailor-made.

So, fasten your seatbelt and get ready to explore the digital landscape. Your small business is about to embark on a journey of discovery, growth, and success. The adventure begins here, and we're excited to be your guides. Together, we'll unlock "The Power of Social Media Marketing for Small Business Growth."

Chapter 2
Defining Your Social Media Strategy

Social media having a strategy is akin to having a roadmap for your journey. It's your guiding light, the plan that ensures every action you take on social media is purposeful and aligned with your business goals. This chapter will delve deep into defining your social media strategy. By the end of it, you'll have a clear blueprint to navigate the social media cosmos effectively.

Setting Clear Objectives

Every successful venture begins with a clear objective in mind. Similarly, your social media strategy should start with well-defined goals. What are your goals with your social media endeavors? Are you striving to enhance brand recognition, steer web traffic, create potential leads, or amplify sales?

Your objectives should be specific, measurable, achievable, relevant, and time-bound (SMART). For example, instead of saying, "I want more followers, you could set an objective like, "I aim to increase my Instagram followers by 20% in the next three months."

Choosing the Right Platforms

The social media landscape is vast, with platforms catering to various demographics and interests. Not all platforms will be suitable for your business. It's essential to identify where your target audience spends their time.

Here's a quick overview of some popular social media platforms and their key demographics:

Facebook: A broad user base suits businesses targeting a diverse audience.

Instagram: Ideal for businesses with visually appealing products or services and a younger audience.

Twitter: Great for real-time updates, news, and engaging with a tech-savvy audience.

LinkedIn: Perfect for B2B businesses and professional networking.

Pinterest: Effective for fashion, home decor, and DIY niche businesses.

YouTube: Excellent for video content and reaching a global audience.

TikTok: Emerging as a powerful platform for short, engaging videos, particularly among younger users.

Understanding Your Audience

You need to understand your audience to tailor your social media strategy effectively. What are their demographics? What interests, difficulties, and aspirations are they driven by? In what ways can your products or services fulfil their requirements?

Creating buyer personas can be incredibly helpful.
A buyer persona is a partly fictional portrayal of your perfect customer, encompassing age, gender, occupation, interests, and difficulties they face. Knowing your audience inside out lets you craft content and messaging that resonates deeply with them.

Content Strategy

Content forms the foundation of your social media strategy, as it captivates your audience, fosters trust and propels them toward your goals. Your content must be in harmony with your brand's tone, principles, and your audience's preferences.

Consider the types of content you'll create:

Posts: can include images, text, or a combination of both. Share updates, news, stories, and educational content.

Videos: Video content is becoming increasingly popular. It can range from short clips to longer-form content like webinars or tutorials.

Images: Visual content often performs well. Use high-quality images that reflect your brand.

User-Generated Content (UGC): Inspire customers to share their encounters with your products or services. UGC fosters trustworthiness and genuineness.

Blogs and Articles: If you have a blog, promote your articles on social media to drive traffic and establish authority in your niche.

Infographics: These are great for presenting complex information visually appealingly.

Polls and Surveys: Involve your audience by requesting their viewpoints or input.

Creating a Content Calendar

Consistency is critical to social media success. Creating a content calendar is essential to maintain a steady presence and engage your audience. This calendar outlines what you'll post and when.

Consider the following when creating your content calendar:

Posting frequency: How often will you post? It's better to post consistently rather than sporadically.

Content themes: What topics will you cover? Plan a mix of promotional content, educational content, and community engagement.

Holidays and events: Incorporate relevant holidays and events into your calendar. These can be great opportunities for themed content.

Analytics and optimization: Regularly review your social media analytics to see what's working and what's not. Adjust your calendar based on these insights.

Chapter 3
Content Creation Mastery

Content is king. It's the currency of the internet, the reason people scroll, click, like, share, and engage. The content draws your audience in, keeps them captivated, and ultimately drives them to take action. In this chapter, we'll explore the art of content creation and equip you with the skills to craft compelling and shareable content that resonates with your target audience.

The Essence of Compelling Content

Compelling content is the secret sauce that turns casual observers into dedicated followers and loyal customers. So, what makes content genuinely effective?

Relevance: Your content should address your target audience's interests, needs, and pain points. It should provide value or entertainment that aligns with their preferences.

Authenticity: Authenticity breeds trust. Be genuine in your content, and let your brand's personality shine. Authentic content is relatable and human, making it more engaging.

Visual Appeal: Visual components like top-notch images, info graphics, and videos can enhance your content's visual allure and share ability.

Storytelling: We're hardwired to respond to stories. Craft narratives that connect with your audience emotionally and effectively convey your brand's message.

Variety: Diversify your content to keep your audience engaged. This can include educational posts, behind-the-scenes glimpses, customer testimonials, and more.

Understanding Your Content Strategy

Before delving into content generation, ensuring that your content harmonizes with your comprehensive social media strategy and business objectives is imperative. Your content strategy should take into account the following components:

Audience Segmentation: Tailor your content to different segments of your audience. For example, you might have content designed for first-time customers, loyal customers, or prospects.

Content Pillars: Identify core themes or topics that resonate with your brand and audience. These content pillars will guide your content creation efforts.

Content Calendar: Plan your content using a content calendar. This ensures consistency and allows you to align content with important dates, events, or product launches.

Content Formats: Determine the types of content you'll create. This can include blog posts, videos, podcasts, infographics, and more.

Content Guidelines: Establish clear tone, style, and branding guidelines to maintain consistency across all content.

Crafting Engaging Written Content

Written content forms the backbone of many social media posts, blogs, and articles. To create engaging written content, keep the following principles in mind:

Clarity: Maintain clear and concise writing with brief sentences and paragraphs, and refrain from using complex jargon or excessively technical terms.

Hook Your Audience: Start with an attention-grabbing headline or opening sentence. Your audience should know what to expect and why they should keep reading.

Tell a Story: Incorporate storytelling elements to make your content more relatable and memorable.

Emphasize Benefits: Highlight the benefits of your products or services. Explain how they solve your audience's problems or improve their lives.

Use Visuals: Enhance the engagement of your content by incorporating visuals alongside your written material to break up the text.

Creating Engaging Visual Content

Leveraging visual content is an effective means of capturing your audience's interest. Below are some suggestions for crafting captivating graphic material:

High-Quality Images: Invest in high-quality images that showcase your products or services in the best light.

Infographics: Employ infographics to illustrate intricate information in a visually attractive and understandable manner.

Video Content: Leverage the power of video content. Consider creating product demos, tutorials, behind-the-scenes videos, and live streams.

User-Generated Content: Motivate your customers to produce content showcasing your products. Utilize this content to establish trust and authenticity.

Consistent Branding: Maintain a consistent visual style across all your content. Use your brand's colors, fonts, and logo to reinforce brand recognition.

Enhancing SEO

Search engine optimization (SEO) is crucial to boost the visibility of your written content. Consider the following SEO tips:

Keyword Exploration: Pinpoint pertinent keywords and phrases your audience seeks.

Optimize Headings: Use descriptive headings and subheadings that include keywords.

Meta Descriptions: Write compelling meta descriptions for your blog posts and articles to entice clicks from search engine results pages.

Internal and External Links:

Incorporate internal links to create associations with other pertinent pages on your website, and include links to credible sources from outside your site.

Mobile-Friendly Adaptation: Ensure that your website and content are mobile-friendly, as many users access content on mobile platforms.

By mastering the art of content creation, you'll be able to produce content that engages your audience consistently, tells your brand's story, and drives your social media marketing strategy forward. Whether crafting written, visual, or a combination of both, remember that practice makes perfect, and experimenting with different approaches can lead to exciting discoveries.

Chapter 4
Building and Engaging Your Community

In social media marketing, your audience is more than just a passive group of followers. They are your community, and building and engaging with this community is a cornerstone of your success. This chapter delves into cultivating a thriving social media community, fostering genuine connections, and transforming your audience into loyal brand advocates.

Understanding the Importance of Community

Your social media community is a living, breathing entity. It comprises individuals interested in your brand, products, or services. Nurturing this community is not only about boosting your follower count; it's about creating a space where your audience feels valued, heard, and inspired to engage.

Why is a solid social media community essential for small businesses?

Trust and Loyalty: A supportive community builds trust in your brand. When people feel a sense of belonging, they are likelier to become loyal customers.

Word-of-Mouth Marketing: Content community members become advocates who enthusiastically share their positive experiences with others, driving natural expansion.

Feedback and Improvement: Your community can provide valuable feedback, helping you improve products, services, and the overall customer experience.

Content Creation: User-generated content from your community can be a powerful marketing tool.

Fostering Genuine Connections

Building a community is not about accumulating the most followers; it's about fostering genuine connections. Here's how you can do that:

Engagement: Actively engage with your audience by promptly responding to comments, questions, and messages. Show that you value their input.

Personalization: Use personalization techniques to make your community members feel seen and appreciated. Address them by their names and acknowledge their achievements.

Consistency: Maintain a consistent posting schedule so your community knows when to expect new content.

Authenticity: Be authentic in your interactions. Share behind-the-scenes glimpses, stories, and challenges. Transparency builds trust.

Empowerment: Empower your community to take ownership. Please encourage them to share their experiences, ideas, and stories related to your brand.

Exclusive Content: Offer exclusive content or perks to your community members to reward their loyalty.

Creating a Safe and Inclusive Space

Your community should be a safe and inclusive space where everyone feels welcome. Consider the following tips:

Moderation: Implement community guidelines and moderate discussions to ensure respectful interactions.

Diversity and Inclusion: Celebrate diversity and inclusion within your community. Encourage conversations that respect different perspectives.

Zero Tolerance for Hate: Be clear about your stance on hate speech, harassment, and discrimination. Take swift action against offenders.

Transforming Followers into Advocates

Your ultimate goal is to turn your followers into brand advocates promoting your business. Here's how you can achieve that:

Highlight User-Generated Content (UGC): Share content created by your community members. It not only acknowledges their efforts but also serves as powerful social proof.

Advocate Programs: Establish advocate programs that recognize and reward loyal community members. This can include special discounts, early product access, or even a shoutout.

Encourage Referrals: Encourage your community to refer friends and family. Offer incentives for successful referrals.

Host Community Challenges: Organize challenges or contests that encourage members to showcase their creativity or how they use your products.

Celebrate Milestones: Celebrate milestones, both yours and your community's. Milestones can be the number of followers, years in business, or individual achievements within the community.

Measuring Community Engagement

Measuring the health of your social media community is vital. Metrics to track include:

Engagement Rate: This measures the interaction level on your posts, including likes, comments, and shares.

Community Growth: Monitor the growth rate of your community to gauge its overall health.

Sentiment Analysis: Analyze comments and mentions to understand the sentiment of your community members.

Advocacy Metrics: Track the number of referrals, user-generated content submissions, and mentions from community members.

Retention Rate: Measure how many followers stay engaged with your community over time.

Building and engaging your social media community is an ongoing process that requires genuine care, dedication, and consistency. By fostering meaningful connections, creating a safe and inclusive space, and transforming followers into advocates, you'll grow your small business and create a tribe of passionate supporters who believe in your brand's mission.

Chapter 5
Cracking the Code of Social Media Algorithms

Social media platforms are not just passive bulletin boards where you can post content and expect it to reach your audience organically. They are dynamic ecosystems driven by complex algorithms determining what content appears in users' feeds. In this chapter, we'll uncover the intricacies of social media algorithms and explore strategies to maximize your content's visibility and engagement.

Understanding Social Media Algorithms

Social media algorithms are like the gatekeepers of the digital realm, sorting through the vast ocean of content to deliver what they believe each user wants to see. These algorithms consider various factors when deciding which content to prioritize:

Engagement: Content that receives likes, comments, shares, and clicks is seen as engaging and is more likely to be shown to a broader audience.

Relevance: The algorithm assesses how relevant a piece of content is to the user. This includes their interests, past interactions, and behavior on the platform.

Recency:
Specific algorithms precede current content to inform users about recent news and trends.

Quality: High-quality content, including well-composed images, informative articles, and engaging videos, is favoured by algorithms.

Connection: Algorithms take into account the user's contacts, giving priority to content from friends, family, and close relationships.

Adapting to Algorithm Changes

Social media algorithms are not static; they evolve. Platforms like Facebook, Instagram, and Twitter frequently update their algorithms to improve user experiences and combat spammy or low-quality content. As a small business, it's essential to adapt to these changes. Here's how:

Stay Informed: Keep abreast of algorithm updates by following official announcements from the platforms and trusted industry news sources.

Broaden Your Content Portfolio: Try out various content formats to determine what resonates effectively within the current algorithmic environment.

Engage Authentically: Focus on genuine engagement rather than chasing vanity metrics. Encourage meaningful interactions with your content.

Consistency: Maintain a consistent posting schedule to signal the algorithm that you are an active and reliable user.

Cracking Individual Platform Algorithms

Every social media platform operates on its distinct algorithm; grasping these subtleties can give your content a competitive advantage. Here's a concise summary of crucial platform algorithms:

Facebook: The Facebook algorithm prefers content that initiates substantial interactions and discussions. It also considers the content type that garners user engagement, such as videos or images.

Instagram: Instagram's algorithm considers user behaviour, including how long they spend on the platform and the type of content they engage with. It also prioritizes new content and favours posts with high engagement in the first few minutes.

Twitter: Twitter's algorithm displays content based on relevance to the user. It considers who you follow, past interactions, and trending topics.

LinkedIn: LinkedIn's algorithm values professionally relevant content that sparks discussions. It rewards long-form articles, videos, and posts with high engagement.

YouTube: YouTube's algorithm focuses on watch time and user behaviour. It recommends videos based on what users have watched, liked, and subscribed to.

Strategies to Maximize Visibility

To navigate social media algorithms successfully, consider these strategies:

Know Your Audience: Understand your audience's preferences and tailor your content accordingly.

Quality over Quantity: Focus on creating high-quality, valuable content that encourages engagement.

Encourage Engagement: Prompt your audience to like, comment, share, and tag friends in your posts.

Use Hashtags Strategically: Research and use relevant hashtags to increase discoverability.

Monitor Analytics: Consistently monitor your analytics to assess the performance of your content and adapt your strategy accordingly.

Collaborate and Cross-Promote:
Collaborate with other businesses or influencers within your field to broaden your outreach to new audiences.

Paid Advertising: Contemplate utilizing paid promotion to amplify the visibility of your content and extend your reach to a broader audience.

Understanding and working with social media algorithms is crucial to successful social media marketing for small businesses. By staying informed, adapting to changes, and implementing strategies that align with each platform's algorithm, you can increase your content's reach and engagement, ultimately driving growth for your small business.

Chapter 6
Advertising on Social Media

Social media advertising has become essential for small businesses to reach their target audiences effectively. In this chapter, we'll explore the world of social media advertising, from creating compelling ad campaigns to measuring ROI and how it can help accelerate your small business growth.

Why Social Media Advertising Matters

Social media advertising offers several compelling advantages for small businesses:

Targeted Reach: You can meticulously tailor your advertisements to reach the most pertinent audience, considering demographics, interests, behaviour, and other factors.

Budget-Friendly: Social media advertising has the potential to be more budget-friendly than traditional advertising, enabling you to make the most of your financial resources.

Engagement: Social media platforms encourage user interaction with ads through likes, shares, comments, and direct messages.

Tangible Results: You can track the efficiency of your advertising campaigns, allowing for data-driven adjustments and improvements.

Creating Effective Ad Campaigns

To make the most of social media advertising, you must create ad campaigns that resonate with your target audience. Here are the key steps:

Define Your Goals: Begin by defining your campaign goals. Do you aim to increase website traffic, generate leads, enhance sales, or elevate brand awareness?

Audience Targeting: Leverage the comprehensive targeting features offered by social media platforms to connect with your ideal audience. Refine your audience selection by considering demographics, interests, and behaviors.

Compelling Creatives: Craft attention-grabbing visuals and copy that communicate your message clearly and concisely. A/B test different ad creatives to identify what resonates best with your audience.

Ad Format Selection: Different platforms offer various ad formats, such as image ads, video ads, carousel ads, and more. Choose the design that best suits your campaign goals.

Budgeting and Scheduling: Set your ad budget and schedule to ensure your campaign runs within your financial constraints and at the optimal times.

Ad Placement: Decide where your ads will appear, whether in users' news feeds, Instagram Stories, or other placements. Consider the platform's recommendations for placement.

Ad Copy and Call to Action:
Create persuasive ad text that motivates your audience to engage. Incorporate a distinct call to action (CTA) corresponding to your campaign's goal.

Measuring ROI and Optimization

Measuring your social media advertising efforts' return on investment (ROI) is crucial to ensure you get the best results. Key metrics to track include:

Click-Through Rate (CTR): The portion of individuals who click your ad post-display.

Conversion Rate: The portion of users who successfully perform the intended action, such as purchasing or subscribing to a newsletter.

Cost per Click (CPC): The average cost you pay for each click on your ads

Return on Ad Spend (ROAS): The income your ad campaign generates relative to the expenditure incurred.

Impressions: The count of instances your ad is exhibited to users.

Ad Relevance Score: Some platforms assign a relevance score based on how well your ad resonates with your audience. A higher score generally leads to lower costs.

Engagement Metrics: Monitor likes, shares, comments, and other interactions to gauge audience engagement.

Once you've gathered data, use it to optimize your ad campaigns. Test elements like ad creatives, headlines, and targeting options to improve performance and reduce costs.

Social Media Advertising Platforms

Each social media platform offers its advertising solutions. Here's a brief overview of some of the major players:

Facebook Ads: Ideal for targeting a broad audience and driving website traffic or brand awareness.

Instagram Ads: Great for visual content and reaching a younger audience.

Twitter Ads: Effective for real-time marketing and promoting trending topics.

LinkedIn Ads: Best for B2B businesses and professional networking.

Pinterest Ads: Useful for fashion, home decor, and DIY businesses.

YouTube Ads: Excellent for video content and reaching a global audience.

Advanced Strategies

As you become more proficient in social media advertising, consider advanced strategies such as:

Retargeting: Display ads to users who have previously interacted with your website or content.

Lookalike Audiences: Create new audiences based on the characteristics of your existing customers.

Dynamic Ads: Automatically show personalized content to users based on their past behaviour.

A/B Testing: Continuously experiment with different ad variations to optimize performance.

Social media advertising holds significant potential for small businesses, yet it's crucial to approach it strategically and consistently adjust your strategy in response to data and insights. As you dive into paid social media advertising, you'll unlock the potential to reach a larger and more targeted audience, accelerating your small business's growth in the digital era.

Chapter 7
Influencer Marketing: A Small Business's Secret Weapon

Influencer marketing has emerged as a potent strategy for small businesses to expand their reach, build credibility, and connect with their target audience on a personal level. In this chapter, we'll dive into influencer marketing, exploring how to identify, collaborate with, and leverage influencers to supercharge your small business growth.

The Rise of Influencer Marketing

Influencer marketing partners with credible individuals and a substantial following in a particular niche or industry. These influencers wield power to sway the opinions and behaviours of their engaged followers. As a small business, tapping into this influence can be a game-changer.

Why Influencer Marketing Matters

Here are several reasons why influencer marketing is a secret weapon for small businesses:

Trust and Authenticity: Influencers often have a loyal and trusting audience. When they endorse your product or service, it carries a level of authenticity that traditional advertising can't replicate.

Targeted Reach: You can select influencers whose followers match your target audience, guaranteeing that your message reaches those most inclined to convert.

Content Creation: Influencers act as content creators, capable of producing compelling, top-notch content that presents your products or services in a relatable manner.

Credibility and Social Proof: An endorsement from a respected influencer provides social proof, which can bolster your brand's credibility.

Budget-Friendly: Influencer marketing can offer a more cost-efficient alternative to traditional advertising approaches, which is particularly beneficial for small businesses operating with constrained budgets.

Identifying the Right Influencers

Selecting the right influencers for your small business is crucial. Here's a step-by-step process to identify potential influencers:

Establish Your Objectives: Identify your intended outcomes for influencer marketing. Whether enhancing brand visibility, promoting products, or boosting website traffic, your objectives will guide your choice of influencers.

Understand Your Audience: Know your target audience inside out. What are their interests, demographics, and pain points? This will help you identify influencers who resonate with your audience.

Research Influencers: Leverage influencer discovery tools and social media platforms to locate influencers within your industry. Be sure to consider factors such as their follower count, engagement rates, and the authenticity of their content. a

Analyze Engagement: Look at an influencer's engagement metrics, including likes, comments, shares, and overall interaction with their audience. High engagement indicates an active and engaged community.

Evaluate Authenticity: Scrutinize the influencer's authenticity. Do their posts appear authentic, or do they seem excessively promotional? Establishing authenticity is essential for fostering trust with your audience.

Relevance: Ensure the influencer's content and values align with your brand. Their endorsement should feel natural and credible.

Building Relationships with Influencers

Once you've identified potential influencers, it's essential to build and nurture relationships with them:

Engage Authentically: Reach out to influencers genuinely interested in your product or service. Personalize your approach and express your appreciation for their work.

Clear Communication: Establish expectations, goals, and deliverables from the outset. Generate a formal contract or agreement that clearly outlines the terms of your collaboration.

Provide Creative Freedom: Allow influencers creative freedom to showcase your product or service in a way that resonates with their audience. Influencers know their followers best.

Compensation: Be prepared to compensate influencers fairly for their work, whether through monetary payment, free products, or another mutually agreed-upon arrangement.

Engagement: Encourage influencers to genuinely engage with their audience about your product or service. Authenticity is critical to maintaining their credibility.

Measuring Influencer Marketing Success

Assessing the impact of your influencer marketing campaigns is essential for understanding their effectiveness. Key performance indicators (KPIs) to keep an eye on include:

Engagement Metrics: Monitor likes, comments, shares, and clicks on posts featuring your product or service.

Follower Growth: Keep an eye on your social media follower growth during and after influencer collaborations.

Web Traffic: Analyze the increase in website traffic, mainly from influencer-driven referral links.

Sales and Conversions: Keep tabs on the number of sales or conversions directly linked to the influence of your influencer marketing endeavours.

Brand Mentions: Measure the increase in brand mentions and conversations on social media after a collaboration.

Survey and Feedback: Gather feedback from customers to gauge the impact of influencer marketing on their decision-making process.

Influencer marketing presents a potent resource for small businesses, providing an authentic means to engage with your desired audience and expedite your expansion. As you continue your journey through "The Power of Social Media Marketing for Small Business Growth," consider influencer marketing a valuable strategy to amplify your brand's reach and credibility in the digital age.

Chapter 8
Social Media Analytics: Unveiling the Data Goldmine

In the digital age, data is a goldmine waiting to be explored. Social media platforms offer abundant information regarding your audience, content effectiveness, and overall marketing approach. This chapter delves into social media analytics, exploring how to effectively harness data to refine your small business's marketing strategy.

The Power of Social Media Analytics

Social media analytics gathers, processes, and interprets data from social media platforms to enable informed decision-making. It is an indispensable element within any thriving social media marketing strategy tailored to small businesses. Here's the rationale:

Informed Decision-Making: Data-driven decisions are more likely to lead to successful outcomes. Analytics provide insights into what's working and what's not.

Audience Understanding: Analytics help you understand your audience's behaviour, preferences, and demographics, allowing you to tailor your content and campaigns more effectively.

Content Optimization: You can identify which types of content perform best, enabling you to create more engaging posts.

Return on Investment (ROI): Analytics enable you to assess the ROI of your social media initiatives, facilitating the effective allocation of resources.

Key Social Media Metrics

To make the most of social media analytics, it's crucial to understand the key metrics you should be tracking:

Engagement Metrics: These include likes, comments, shares, and clicks. They indicate how well your content resonates with your audience.

Reach and Impressions: Reach measures how many unique users have seen your content, while impressions indicate the total number of times your content has been viewed.

Follower Growth: Monitor the growth of your social media followers over time. A steady increase is a positive sign.

Click-Through Rate (CTR): CTR quantifies the proportion of users who engage with a link in your post, indicating the efficacy of your call-to-action.

Conversion Rate: This metric monitors the proportion of users who have successfully taken a specific action, like subscribing to a newsletter or making a purchase.

Bounce Rate: Regarding web traffic stemming from social media, the bounce rate quantifies the proportion of users who depart your site after viewing just one page. A substantial bounce rate could suggest potential challenges with your landing pages.

Social Shares: Track how often your content is shared on social media platforms. Shares extend your content's reach.

Social Mentions: Keep a watchful eye on references to your brand across social media platforms, as they can yield valuable insights into public sentiments and opinions about your business.

Tools for Social Media Analytics

Numerous tools and platforms are available to help you analyze social media data effectively. Some popular options include:

Google Analytics: This free tool provides in-depth insights into website traffic, including your social media traffic sources and user behaviour.

Social Media Analytics: Most social media platforms furnish their individualized and dedicated analytical instruments. For instance, Facebook Insights provides data on how your posts perform and your audience's demographic composition.

Hootsuite: A social media management platform with analytics features that allow you to track performance across multiple platforms.

Another social media management tool that supplies analytics and reporting to assist you in evaluating and enhancing your social media strategy.

Sprout Social: A comprehensive social media management and analytics platform that offers in-depth reporting and data visualization.

Using Data to Optimize Your Strategy

Here are steps to effectively use data to optimize your social media marketing strategy:

Set Clear Goals: Establish specific, measurable objectives for your social media campaigns. Your goals will guide your data analysis efforts.

Regularly Review Data: Schedule regular data review sessions to track progress and identify trends.

A/B Testing: Explore various content formats, posting schedules, and tactics to determine which connects most effectively with your audience.

Refine Your Content: Use insights from analytics to refine your content strategy. Concentrate on producing content that matches your audience's tastes and preferences.

Budget Allocation: Analyze the ROI of your social media advertising campaigns to optimize budget allocation.

Competitor Analysis: Study your competitors' social media performance to identify areas where you can improve.

Data-Driven Reporting: Leverage data to generate reports illustrating the influence of your social media endeavours. Emphasize essential metrics and demonstrate how they correspond to your objectives.

Staying Informed and Adapting

The social media landscape constantly evolves, and your analytics strategy should become. Stay informed about updates to social media algorithms, new analytics features, and emerging trends. Adapt your strategy based on data and insights to ensure that your small business remains competitive and continues to grow in the digital realm.

Chapter 9
Customer Relationship Management in the Digital Age

Building and maintaining solid customer relationships is paramount for small business success in the fast-paced digital age. In this chapter, we'll explore the world of Customer Relationship Management (CRM) and how leveraging digital tools and strategies can help you create lasting connections with your audience.

The Importance of Customer Relationship Management

Customer Relationship Management (CRM) strategically focuses on supervising and nurturing customer relationships throughout their entire interaction with your business. In the digital age, characterized by intense competition and many choices for customers, a robust CRM approach can distinguish your small business. Here's why CRM is significant:

Customer Retention: Building solid relationships fosters customer loyalty, reducing churn and increasing lifetime customer value.

Personalization: A well-implemented CRM system lets you personalize your interactions with customers, making them feel valued and understood.

Data-Driven Decisions: CRM tools provide valuable customer data and insights, empowering you to make informed marketing and sales decisions.

Efficiency: Automating and organizing customer interactions streamline your processes, saving time and resources.

Customer Feedback: CRM systems allow you to gather feedback and insights from customers, helping you refine your products, services, and customer experiences.

Implementing a Digital CRM Strategy

Here's how to implement an effective digital CRM strategy for your small business:

Choose the Right CRM Software: Choose a CRM platform that matches your business requirements and financial constraints. Some well-liked choices encompass Sales force, Hub Spot CRM, and Zoho CRM.

Data Collection and Integration: Collect customer information from diverse channels like your website, social media, and email campaigns. Integrate this data into your CRM system to comprehensively understand each buyer.

Segmentation: Categorize your customer base into groups according to demographics, behavior, and purchase history. This enables the customization of messaging and offers.

Personalization: Use CRM data to personalize your marketing messages, emails, and offers. Address customers by name and recommend products or services based on their past interactions.

Automation: Implement automation for routine tasks, such as email follow-ups, appointment scheduling, and customer on boarding.

Lead Management: Use your CRM system to track and manage leads, nurturing them through the sales funnel until they become customers.

Customer Support: Integrate customer support into your CRM to provide timely assistance and track customer inquiries and resolutions.

Building Customer Loyalty Through CRM

A central goal of CRM is to build customer loyalty. Here's how you can achieve this through your digital CRM strategy:

Consistent Communication: Regularly communicate with your customers through email marketing, social media, and personalized messaging.

Value-Added Content: Provide valuable content, such as blog posts, videos, and webinars, that addresses your customers' needs and interests.

Loyalty Programs: Implement loyalty programs or rewards systems to incentivize repeat purchases and referrals.

Feedback and Surveys: Gather customer feedback and act on their suggestions to improve your products or services.

Exceptional Customer Service: Provide outstanding customer service through prompt responses, problem resolution, and a friendly, empathetic approach.

Exclusive Offers: Provide your devoted customers with exclusive promotions or the opportunity for early access to new products or services.

Social Engagement:
- *Engage with your customers on social media.*
- *Respond to their comments and messages.*
- *Celebrate their milestones.*

Measuring CRM Success

To gauge the success of your CRM efforts, track key performance indicators (KPIs) such as:

Customer Retention Rate: The portion of customers who uphold an ongoing business relationship with you over a specified period.

Customer Lifetime Value (CLV): The cumulative revenue customers generate during their complete association with your business.

Net Promoter Score (NPS): Customer satisfaction and loyalty based on their likelihood to recommend your business to others.

Customer Satisfaction (CSAT): A survey-based metric that measures customer satisfaction with your products or services.

Response Time: The duration required to reply to customer queries or support requests.

Conversion Rate: The proportion of potential leads that transform into paying customers.

A well-executed digital CRM strategy can transform your small business by fostering strong customer relationships, increasing customer loyalty, and ultimately driving growth. As you continue your journey through "The Power of Social Media Marketing for Small Business Growth," remember that the digital age offers unprecedented opportunities to connect with your audience personally. You can create meaningful, lasting connections that set your business apart by leveraging CRM tools and strategies.

Chapter 10
E-commerce Strategies for Small Business Growth

E-commerce has transformed businesses' operations, providing small companies with new avenues for growth and expansion.
This chapter will delve into e-commerce strategies specifically designed for small businesses, covering everything from establishing an online store to enhancing your digital storefront for optimal results.

The E-commerce Revolution

E-commerce has become a driving force in the business world, offering a wealth of opportunities for small businesses:

Global Reach: E-commerce enables you to reach customers locally, nationally, and internationally.

Lower Overheads: Operating an online store often requires fewer overhead costs than a brick-and-mortar establishment.

Convenience: E-commerce offers customers the convenience of shopping from anywhere, any time, leading to increased sales potential.

Data-Driven Insights: E-commerce platforms provide valuable data on customer behaviour, allowing for more targeted marketing efforts.

Setting Up Your Online Store

Launching an online store requires careful planning and execution. Here's a step-by-step guide to get you started:

Choose an E-commerce Platform: Select an e-commerce platform that aligns with your business needs. Popular options include Shopify, Woo Commerce (for WordPress users), and Big Commerce

.

Domain Name: Secure a domain name that mirrors your brand and is simple for customers to recall.

Website Design: Invest in a visually appealing, user-friendly, mobile-responsive professional website design.

Product Listings: Create detailed product listings with high-quality images, compelling descriptions, and pricing information.

Shopping Cart and Checkout: Ensure a seamless shopping experience by implementing a user-friendly shopping cart and checkout process.

Payment Processing: Set up secure payment processing options, including credit card payments, digital wallets, and other popular methods.

Shipping and Fulfillment: Determine your shipping strategy, including shipping rates and delivery times. Choose a reliable fulfilment method, whether in-house or outsourced.

Security: Prioritize website security to protect customer data and build trust. Use SSL certificates and secure payment gateways.

Digital Marketing for E-commerce

To succeed in the competitive e-commerce landscape, you'll need effective digital marketing strategies:

Search Engine Optimization (SEO): Enhance your product listings and website content to achieve better rankings in search engine results pages (SERPs).

Social Media Advertising: Utilize paid advertising on platforms like Facebook, Instagram, and Google Ads to reach your target audience.

Content Marketing: Create valuable content that addresses customer pain points and educates them about your products or industry.

Email Marketing: Establish an email list and dispatch focused email campaigns to connect with your customers, promote products, and furnish updates.

Influencer Marketing: Collaborate with influencers within your sector to have them promote your products to their highly engaged audience.

Customer Reviews and Testimonials: Encourage satisfied customers to leave reviews and testimonials, boosting trust and credibility.

Retargeting: Integrate retargeting advertisements to rekindle the interest of potential customers who have displayed interest in your products but still need to complete a purchase.

Data-Driven Decision-Making

E-commerce platforms provide a wealth of data that can inform your business decisions:

Sales Metrics: Monitor sales, conversion rates, and average order values to assess the performance of your online store.

Customer Behavior: Analyze customer behaviour, such as page views, time spent on site, and abandoned carts, to identify opportunities for improvement.

Inventory Management: Use data to optimize inventory levels and avoid overstocking products.

Customer Segmentation: Segment your customer base based on buying habits, demographics, and preferences to tailor marketing campaigns.

A/B Testing: Perform trials with different elements on your website, such as product descriptions or images, to discover what connects most powerfully with your audience.

Return on Investment (ROI): Calculate the ROI of your digital marketing efforts to ensure you're allocating resources effectively.

Adapting and Scaling

E-commerce is a dynamic field that requires adaptability and scalability:

Stay Informed: Keep up with e-commerce trends, new technologies, and changes in customer behaviour.

Scalability: Be prepared to scale your operations as your business grows. This may involve expanding your product line, reaching new markets, or optimizing your supply chain.

Customer Support: Offer exceptional customer assistance through various communication avenues, encompassing live chat, email, and phone, to address customer inquiries and resolve their concerns promptly.

Security: Continually update and strengthen your website's security measures to protect customer data.

Feedback Loop: Encourage customer feedback and use it to improve your products, services, and overall shopping experience.

E-commerce presents boundless opportunities for small businesses to thrive in the digital age. By strategically setting up your online store, implementing effective digital marketing tactics, and leveraging data-driven insights, you can position your small business for growth and success in the competitive e-commerce landscape.

Conclusion

Harnessing the Power of Social Media for Small Business Growth

In the ever-evolving landscape of the digital age, small businesses face unprecedented challenges and boundless opportunities. As we conclude our journey through "The Power of Social Media Marketing for Small Business Growth," it's clear that harnessing the potential of social media is not just a strategy; it's a lifeline for success in today's competitive world.

Throughout these pages, we've explored the dynamic realm of social media marketing, uncovering insights, strategies, and techniques tailored to the unique needs of small businesses. We've witnessed the transformational impact that social media can have on your brand's visibility, engagement, and, ultimately, your bottom line.

We've discussed the importance of crafting compelling narratives, building authentic connections, and narrating your distinctive report in a manner that strikes a chord with your audience. We've navigated the complexities of social media algorithms, learning how to adapt to their ever-changing algorithms to ensure your content reaches the right people at the right time.

We've delved into the world of paid advertising, discovering how to leverage the precision of targeting and the magic of creativity to maximize the ROI of your ad campaigns. We've unlocked the potential of influencer marketing, understanding how to collaborate with individuals who can amplify your message and lend their credibility to your brand.

We've unravelled the mysteries of social media analytics, turning data into insights that drive informed decisions and propel your strategies forward. We've embraced the power of Customer

Relationship Management (CRM), fostering lasting connections with your customers that transcend transactions and build brand loyalty.

And finally, we've embarked on the e-commerce revolution, exploring how small businesses can thrive in the digital age by setting up online stores, embracing digital marketing, and using data to adapt and scale their operations.

But beyond the strategies and tactics, the true essence of social media marketing for small businesses lies in a mindset. This mindset champions creativity, adaptability, and the relentless pursuit of excellence. It's about understanding that social media is not just a tool but a platform for storytelling, community-building, and making a real impact in your customers' lives.

Remember that the path to success is not always linear in the journey ahead. You may encounter challenges and setbacks, but these are opportunities to learn, grow, and refine your approach. Embrace experimentation, seek out innovation, and always keep sight of the unique value you bring.

As a small business owner, you are part of a vibrant and resilient community that thrives on passion, determination, and a relentless pursuit of dreams. "The Power of Social Media Marketing for Small Business Growth" has been your guide, but the journey is yours to continue. With the knowledge, strategies, and inspiration found within these pages, you have the tools to create a future where your small business survives and thrives.

So, go forth with confidence, courage, and creativity. Embrace the limitless possibilities of social media, and remember that the power to shape your business's destiny is in your hands. May your journey be filled with growth, impact, and the fulfilment of your greatest aspirations.